Mastering Manage:
Economics: Unleashing
Behavior

Julia

Title: Mastering Management with Behavioral Economics: Unleashing the Power of Human Behavior

Author's: Julia.

This book was printed and published by [Publisher's: Julia] in [2023]

ISBN:

TABLE OF CONTENTS

Chapter 7: Behavioral Economics in Consumer Behavior and Marketing

Understanding Consumer Decision Making

The Influence of Behavioral Economics in Marketing Strategies

Nudging Consumers towards Desired Purchases

Chapter 8: Ethical Considerations in Behavioral Economics and Management

Ethical Implications of Nudging in Organizations

Ensuring Fairness and Transparency in Behavioral Economics Strategies

Balancing Ethical Concerns with Organizational Objectives

Chapter 9: Implementing Behavioral Economics in Organizational Practices

Building a Behavioral Economics Framework in Organizations

Strategies for Integrating Behavioral Economics into Management Processes

Overcoming Challenges in Implementing Behavioral Economics

Chapter 1: Introduction to Behavioral Economics in Organizational Behavior and Management

What is Behavioral Economics?

Behavioral Economics is a fascinating field that combines insights from psychology and economics to understand and predict human behavior in decision-making processes. It delves into the intricacies of why people make certain choices, often deviating from traditional economic theories that assume individuals are consistently rational and always act in their best interest.

This subchapter aims to provide an overview of Behavioral Economics, shedding light on its fundamental concepts and principles. Whether you are a student, a business professional, or simply curious about human behavior, understanding Behavioral Economics can offer valuable insights into how individuals and societies make decisions.

At its core, Behavioral Economics recognizes that humans are prone to biases, cognitive limitations, and emotions that influence their choices. It challenges the traditional economic assumption that individuals always act rationally by exploring the various factors that impact decision-making, such as social influences, heuristics, and framing effects.

By studying Behavioral Economics, you will gain a deeper understanding of why people often make seemingly irrational choices. For instance, why do we tend to overestimate our abilities? Why do we prefer avoiding losses rather than acquiring equivalent gains? These questions and more will be answered as we explore the fascinating world of behavioral economics.

Throughout this subchapter, we will delve into key theories and experiments that have shaped the field of Behavioral Economics. We will explore concepts like prospect theory, which explains how people evaluate and make decisions under uncertainty, and the endowment effect, which describes our tendency to value objects we own more than identical objects that we do not own.

Additionally, we will discuss the practical applications of Behavioral Economics in various domains, such as marketing, finance, and public policy. By understanding the underlying mechanisms that drive human behavior, you will be better equipped to design effective strategies, influence consumer choices, and drive positive change.

In conclusion, Behavioral Economics is a powerful tool that uncovers the intricacies of human decision-making. By combining insights from psychology and economics, this field offers a fresh perspective on why people behave the way they do. Whether you are interested in personal development, business success, or societal change, mastering Behavioral Economics will empower you to unleash the power of human behavior. So, let's embark on this exciting journey together and unlock the secrets of decision-making!

Why Behavioral Economics is Relevant in Management

Management is an essential aspect of any organization, and it plays a crucial role in determining its success or failure. Traditional management theories have long focused on rational decision-making and assumed that people are entirely rational in their choices. However, the field of behavioral economics has emerged as a powerful tool in understanding and influencing human behavior, making it increasingly relevant in the context of management.

Behavioral economics combines insights from psychology and economics to explain and predict human behavior, recognizing that individuals are not always rational in their decision-making. This field acknowledges that people are influenced by cognitive biases, emotions, and social factors, which can impact their choices and actions in the workplace. By understanding these behavioral patterns, managers can make informed decisions and devise effective strategies to optimize organizational performance.

One of the most significant contributions of behavioral economics to management is its understanding of motivation. Traditional economic theories assume that individuals are solely driven by financial incentives. However, behavioral economics recognizes that people are motivated by a complex set of factors, including social recognition, autonomy, and purpose. By leveraging this understanding, managers can design incentive programs that align with employees' intrinsic motivations, leading to higher engagement and productivity.

Additionally, behavioral economics sheds light on decision-making biases that individuals exhibit, such as loss aversion, confirmation bias, and overconfidence. Managers can use this knowledge to mitigate these biases and improve decision-making processes within the organization. For example, by encouraging diverse perspectives and creating an environment that promotes critical thinking, managers can prevent groupthink and improve the quality of decisions made by teams.

Furthermore, behavioral economics offers insights into the importance of framing and presentation in influencing behavior. By understanding how individuals perceive and process information, managers can effectively communicate their goals and objectives, ensuring clarity and alignment. This can help build a shared vision and enhance employee commitment towards organizational goals.

In conclusion, behavioral economics brings a fresh perspective to management by acknowledging the complexities of human behavior. By understanding and utilizing the principles of behavioral economics, managers can optimize decision-making, motivate employees, and shape a positive organizational culture. With its focus on the power of human behavior, behavioral economics has become an indispensable tool for effective management in today's dynamic and diverse workplace.

Understanding Human Behavior in Organizations

In the dynamic world of business, organizations are constantly striving to achieve success and maintain a competitive edge. However, one crucial factor that often determines the fate of an organization is the behavior of the individuals within it. To effectively manage and lead an organization, it is essential to understand human behavior in the context of the workplace. This subchapter will delve into the intricacies of understanding human behavior in organizations, utilizing the principles of behavioral economics.

Behavioral economics is a field that combines insights from psychology and economics to understand why individuals make certain decisions and how their behavior can be influenced. By applying these principles to the study of human behavior in organizations, we can gain valuable insights into the dynamics that drive employee performance, motivation, and decision-making.

In this subchapter, we will explore various aspects of human behavior in organizations. We will examine the role of motivation and how it can be harnessed to enhance employee performance. We will delve into the impact of organizational culture on behavior, highlighting the importance of fostering a positive and inclusive work environment. Additionally, we will explore the role of leadership in shaping employee behavior and the strategies managers can employ to create a productive and engaged workforce.

Furthermore, this subchapter will also shed light on the factors that influence decision-making within organizations. We will discuss the role of biases and heuristics in shaping employee choices and how these can lead to suboptimal decision-making. By understanding these cognitive biases, managers can design systems and processes that mitigate their effects and promote rational decision-making.

The insights gained from understanding human behavior in organizations can significantly impact the success of an organization. By recognizing the underlying motivations and biases that drive employee behavior, managers can create strategies and interventions that promote a positive work culture, enhance employee engagement, and drive organizational performance.

Whether you are a business owner, manager, or an employee seeking to understand the dynamics of organizational behavior, this subchapter will provide you with valuable insights and practical knowledge. By harnessing the power of behavioral economics, you can unlock the potential of human behavior in organizations and propel your business to new heights of success.

Chapter 2: Behavioral Economics Principles in Employee Motivation

The Rationality Assumption and Motivation

In the world of behavioral economics, the rationality assumption is a fundamental concept that explores how individuals make decisions. It is based on the belief that people are rational beings who consistently make choices that maximize their own self-interest. However, this assumption fails to capture the complexities of human behavior and motivation.

Motivation is a powerful force that drives our actions and decisions. It is influenced by various factors, such as emotions, social norms, and biases. Understanding the interplay between rationality and motivation is crucial for mastering management and harnessing the power of human behavior.

Contrary to the rationality assumption, research in behavioral economics has shown that individuals often make decisions that deviate from logical or self-interested behavior. Emotions, for instance, can override rational thinking and lead to impulsive choices. Similarly, social norms and peer pressure can influence decision-making, causing individuals to conform to the behavior of others, even if it goes against their self-interest.

Motivation is also closely tied to biases, which are systematic errors in thinking that affect our judgment. Cognitive biases, such as confirmation bias or loss aversion, can lead individuals to make irrational decisions. These biases stem from our inherent need to simplify complex information and rely on mental shortcuts, which can often lead to flawed reasoning.

Recognizing the limitations of the rationality assumption is essential for managers in order to effectively motivate and influence their teams. By understanding the underlying factors that drive behavior, managers can design incentives and structures that align with employees' motivations. For instance, instead of relying solely on financial rewards, managers can leverage intrinsic motivations, such as autonomy, mastery, and purpose, to foster engagement and productivity.

Furthermore, managers must be aware of the biases that can impact decision-making within their teams. By creating an environment that encourages open dialogue and diverse perspectives, managers can mitigate the influence of biases and promote more rational decision-making.

In summary, the rationality assumption in behavioral economics fails to capture the complexities of human behavior and motivation. Motivation, driven by emotions, social norms, and biases, plays a significant role in decision-making. Understanding this interplay is crucial for mastering management and leveraging the power of human behavior. By acknowledging the limitations of rationality and designing strategies that align with individuals' motivations, managers can create a more effective and productive work environment.

Incentives and Rewards: The Power of Behavioral Economics

In the world of management and decision-making, understanding human behavior is crucial. Why do people make certain choices? How can we motivate individuals to perform at their best? These questions lie at the heart of behavioral economics, a field that combines psychology and economics to uncover the underlying drivers of human behavior.

Incentives and rewards play a pivotal role in shaping our actions and behaviors. Traditional economic theory assumes that individuals are rational and always act in their best self-interest. However, behavioral economics challenges this assumption by recognizing that humans are not always rational beings. Instead, we are often driven by cognitive biases and emotional responses that influence our decision-making.

By leveraging the principles of behavioral economics, managers can harness the power of incentives and rewards to shape behavior and drive desired outcomes. This subchapter explores the various ways in which incentives and rewards can be used effectively to motivate individuals and enhance performance.

One of the key insights from behavioral economics is that the way incentives are framed can have a significant impact on behavior. Research has shown that people tend to be more motivated by gains than losses. Therefore, framing incentives as rewards rather than penalties can be more effective in driving desired behaviors.

Moreover, the timing and delivery of incentives also matter. Behavioral economists have found that immediate rewards are more powerful in driving behavior change than delayed ones. By providing instant gratification, managers can tap into the human tendency for instant rewards and increase motivation.

Additionally, the concept of social norms and peer influence is vital in behavioral economics. People are highly influenced by what others around them are doing. Incorporating social incentives and rewards, such as public recognition or team-based rewards, can foster a sense of competition and camaraderie, leading to increased motivation and performance.

However, it is crucial to understand that incentives and rewards are not a one-size-fits-all solution. Each individual is unique, and what motivates one person may not work for another. Therefore, managers should consider tailoring incentives and rewards to individual preferences and needs, taking into account factors such as personality traits, cultural backgrounds, and personal goals.

In conclusion, incentives and rewards have the power to shape behavior and enhance performance in the workplace. By understanding the principles of behavioral economics, managers can design effective incentive systems that tap into human motivations and drive desired outcomes. However, it is essential to consider individual differences and preferences when implementing these strategies. Behavioral economics offers a powerful toolkit for mastering management and unleashing the full potential of human behavior.

Nudging Employees towards Desired Behaviors

Subchapter: Nudging Employees towards Desired Behaviors

Introduction:
In today's fast-paced and competitive business environment, it is essential for organizations to align their employees' behaviors with the desired outcomes. However, traditional management techniques often fall short in achieving this goal. This is where behavioral economics comes into play, offering powerful insights into human behavior and providing effective strategies for influencing employees' actions. In this subchapter, we will explore how managers can utilize the principles of behavioral economics to nudge their employees towards desired behaviors, fostering a more productive and motivated workforce.

Understanding   Behavioral   Economics:
Behavioral economics combines psychology and economics to analyze how individuals make decisions and behave in real-world situations. It recognizes that people are not always rational and that their decisions are influenced by various psychological factors. By understanding these factors, managers can design interventions that encourage employees to make choices aligned with organizational goals.

Choice   Architecture:
One of the key concepts in behavioral economics is choice architecture, which refers to the way choices are presented to individuals. By carefully designing the work environment and framing options, managers can influence employees' decisions. For example,

placing healthy snacks at eye level in the office pantry can encourage healthier eating habits among employees.

Using   Incentives:
Incentives play a crucial role in shaping behavior. However, traditional monetary incentives are not always the most effective option. Behavioral economics suggests that non-monetary incentives, such as recognition, social status, or even gamification, can be more motivating for employees. By understanding what truly motivates their workforce, managers can design incentive systems that encourage desired behaviors.

Default   Options:
Default options have a significant impact on employees' decisions. By setting default options that align with the desired behavior, managers can make it easier for employees to make the right choices. For instance, setting email filters that prioritize important tasks can nudge employees towards better time management.

Social   Norms   and   Peer   Influence:
Humans are social creatures, and their behavior is heavily influenced by social norms and peer pressure. Managers can leverage this by creating a work culture that promotes desired behaviors and encourages employees to hold each other accountable. By highlighting positive role models and fostering a sense of community, managers can harness the power of social influence to drive behavior change.

Conclusion:
Mastering management with behavioral economics allows managers to understand the underlying drivers of human behavior and use them

to their advantage. By aligning employees' behaviors with organizational goals, managers can create a more productive and motivated workforce. By employing choice architecture, incentives, default options, and leveraging social norms, managers can effectively nudge employees towards desired behaviors, leading to improved performance and organizational success.

Chapter 3: Behavioral Economics in Decision Making and Problem Solving

Cognitive Biases and Decision Making

In the fascinating realm of Behavioral Economics, understanding the intricate relationship between cognitive biases and decision making is crucial. As human beings, we like to think of ourselves as rational decision-makers, carefully weighing all available information before arriving at a well-reasoned choice. However, the reality is far from this ideal. Our decisions are often influenced by a multitude of biases, which can lead to less than optimal outcomes.

Cognitive biases are systematic errors in our thinking process that arise from the limits of our cognitive abilities. These biases can affect our perception, judgment, and decision-making abilities, often leading to irrational and flawed choices. By recognizing and understanding these biases, we can minimize their impact and make more informed decisions.

One prominent cognitive bias is the confirmation bias, where we seek out information that supports our existing beliefs and ignore or dismiss contradictory evidence. This bias can lead to a narrow-minded decision-making process, as we fail to consider all available perspectives and information. Overcoming this bias requires actively seeking out different viewpoints and challenging our own assumptions.

Another common cognitive bias is the availability heuristic, where we rely on immediate examples that come to mind when making judgments. This bias can lead to overlooking important information and relying on stereotypes or preconceived notions. To counter this bias, we need to gather and analyze comprehensive data, rather than relying solely on what is readily available.

The anchoring bias, on the other hand, refers to our tendency to rely heavily on the first piece of information we receive when making decisions. This bias can distort our judgment, as subsequent information is often evaluated in relation to this initial anchor. To mitigate the impact of anchoring bias, it is essential to consider multiple sources of information and critically evaluate each piece of data.

Understanding and addressing these cognitive biases can significantly enhance our decision-making abilities. By consciously challenging our assumptions, seeking diverse perspectives, and ensuring we have a comprehensive understanding of the available information, we can make more rational and informed choices.

In the world of management, being aware of cognitive biases is particularly important. Leaders must make critical decisions that can have far-reaching consequences for their organizations. By incorporating the principles of behavioral economics into management practices, leaders can foster a culture of critical thinking and evidence-based decision-making, ultimately leading to more successful outcomes.

In conclusion, cognitive biases play a significant role in decision making, and understanding their impact is crucial for anyone interested in Behavioral Economics. By recognizing and addressing these biases, we can enhance our decision-making abilities and make more rational choices. Incorporating these insights into management practices can lead to more effective leadership and better organizational outcomes. So, let us embark on this journey of mastering management with behavioral economics and unleash the power of human behavior.

Prospect Theory and Risk Preferences

In the fascinating world of behavioral economics, one of the most influential theories is Prospect Theory. Developed by psychologists Daniel Kahneman and Amos Tversky in the 1970s, Prospect Theory challenges traditional assumptions about human decision-making and risk preferences. Understanding this theory can unlock a whole new perspective on how we make choices and perceive risks.

Prospect Theory suggests that people do not always make rational decisions based on absolute outcomes, but rather evaluate choices relative to a reference point. This reference point can be influenced by various factors, such as past experiences, social norms, or even immediate circumstances. For example, if an individual receives a bonus at work, they may perceive a subsequent loss of the same amount as more significant and upsetting than if they had not received the bonus. This is known as the "loss aversion" aspect of Prospect Theory.

Another critical element of Prospect Theory is the concept of diminishing sensitivity to gains and losses. It suggests that people are less sensitive to changes when they are already in a positive or negative state. For instance, the difference between gaining $10 and gaining $20 feels more significant than the difference between gaining $110 and gaining $120. Similarly, losing $10 when already in a negative state feels less painful than losing $10 when in a neutral state. This phenomenon helps explain why individuals often take more risks to recover from losses.

When it comes to risk preferences, Prospect Theory challenges the traditional economic notion that individuals always seek to maximize expected utility. According to Prospect Theory, individuals are more risk-averse when facing gains and more risk-seeking when facing losses. This preference for risk-taking during losses can be attributed to the idea of "losses loom larger than gains" – the fear of missing out on an opportunity to recover from a loss.

Understanding Prospect Theory and its implications can have profound effects on various aspects of our lives. It can shed light on why individuals may be more inclined to invest in risky ventures when trying to recoup losses. Additionally, it can help explain why people are more likely to buy insurance for smaller risks but avoid it for larger ones – the fear of incurring a loss in the future.

By recognizing the influence of Prospect Theory on our decision-making processes, we can make more informed choices and better manage our risk preferences. This knowledge is valuable not only for individuals but also for businesses, policymakers, and professionals in various fields. Mastering the insights of Prospect Theory can unleash the power of human behavior, leading to more effective strategies, policies, and overall decision-making processes.

Framing Effects in Decision Making

In the world of decision making, our choices are often influenced by external factors that we may not even be aware of. One such factor is known as framing effects, which play a crucial role in shaping our decisions. Understanding these effects is essential for anyone who wants to master management in today's complex world. In this subchapter, we will delve into the fascinating realm of framing effects and how they can be harnessed to unleash the power of human behavior.

Framing effects, in the context of behavioral economics, refer to the way in which the presentation or framing of information can significantly influence the decisions we make. Our choices are not solely based on the objective value or utility of the options presented to us; rather, they are heavily influenced by how the options are framed. This phenomenon has been extensively studied and has profound implications for individuals, businesses, and societies as a whole.

One common framing effect is the distinction between gains and losses. When presented with a choice, individuals tend to be risk-averse when the options are framed in terms of potential gains. Conversely, when the options are framed as potential losses, individuals become more risk-seeking. This effect can have significant consequences in various domains, such as investment decisions, marketing strategies, and public policy.

Another framing effect revolves around the concept of reference points. People tend to evaluate outcomes based on a reference point, which can be influenced by the way information is presented. For example, if a product is initially priced high and then discounted, consumers may perceive the discount as a gain. On the other hand, if the product is initially priced low and then increased, consumers may perceive the price increase as a loss. Understanding how reference points shape our decisions can help managers design effective pricing strategies and promotional campaigns.

Furthermore, framing effects can also be used to nudge individuals towards making certain choices. By carefully framing the options, managers can steer decision-making in a desired direction without imposing explicit constraints. This technique, known as choice architecture, has been successfully employed in various domains, including healthcare, finance, and environmental conservation.

Mastering the art of framing effects in decision making is an invaluable skill for managers and individuals alike. By understanding how these effects shape our choices, we can make more informed decisions, design effective strategies, and ultimately unleash the power of human behavior. In the next chapters, we will explore practical examples and case studies that demonstrate the real-world applications of framing effects in behavioral economics. So, buckle up and get ready to uncover the secrets behind the fascinating world of decision-making biases and how they can be leveraged to achieve desired outcomes.

Overcoming Biases for Effective Problem Solving

In today's fast-paced and complex world, effective problem solving is a crucial skill for success in every aspect of life. Whether you are a business leader, a student, or a stay-at-home parent, the ability to find innovative solutions to challenges can make a significant difference in achieving your goals. However, our human nature often leads us astray with biases that hinder our problem-solving abilities. This subchapter aims to explore the concept of overcoming biases through the lens of behavioral economics, empowering every individual to master the art of effective problem solving.

Behavioral economics is a field that combines psychology and economics to understand how individuals make decisions and evaluate risks and rewards. It offers valuable insights into the biases that influence our thinking patterns and decision-making processes. By identifying and overcoming these biases, we can enhance our problem-solving skills and make more rational and informed choices.

One of the most common biases we encounter is confirmation bias. This bias leads us to seek information that supports our existing beliefs and ignore or dismiss evidence to the contrary. To overcome this bias, it is crucial to actively seek out diverse perspectives and challenge our own assumptions. Engaging in open-minded discussions and considering alternative viewpoints can help us see the bigger picture and uncover new insights that may lead to innovative solutions.

Another bias that frequently hampers effective problem solving is anchoring bias. This bias occurs when we rely too heavily on the first piece of information we encounter when making decisions. To overcome anchoring bias, it is essential to gather a wide range of information and evaluate it objectively. By considering multiple sources and viewpoints, we can avoid fixating on a single idea or solution and explore a broader range of possibilities.

Furthermore, availability bias is a bias that influences our judgment based on how easily we can recall relevant examples or information. To overcome this bias, we should actively seek out additional information and consider a more comprehensive range of examples. By expanding our knowledge base and considering a wider array of possibilities, we can make more accurate and effective decisions in problem-solving situations.

By understanding and actively working to overcome biases, we can unlock the full potential of our problem-solving abilities. Behavioral economics offers valuable insights and tools to help us navigate the complex terrain of decision-making. By embracing a more open-minded and rational approach, we can unleash the power of human behavior to achieve success in all areas of life. So, let us embark on this journey together, empowering ourselves to become exceptional problem solvers.

Chapter 4: Applying Behavioral Economics to Leadership and Teamwork

Behavioral Economics and Leadership Styles

Leadership is a critical aspect of management that plays a pivotal role in the success or failure of organizations. However, traditional management theories often overlook the impact of human behavior on leadership styles. This is where the emerging field of behavioral economics comes into play, offering valuable insights into understanding and improving leadership styles.

Behavioral economics is a discipline that combines insights from psychology and economics to analyze how individuals make decisions. By understanding the biases, heuristics, and cognitive limitations that influence decision-making, we can gain a deeper understanding of leadership styles and their effectiveness.

One of the key principles of behavioral economics is that humans are not always rational decision-makers. This has significant implications for leadership styles. Traditional leadership theories often assume a rational and logical decision-making process, but in reality, leaders and their subordinates are influenced by a range of cognitive biases and emotions.

For example, the availability bias leads leaders to make decisions based on the most readily available information, rather than considering all relevant data. This can result in poor decision-making and suboptimal leadership outcomes. By being aware of these biases, leaders can adopt strategies to mitigate their impact and make more informed decisions.

Another important concept in behavioral economics is loss aversion. This bias suggests that individuals tend to be more motivated by avoiding losses than by achieving gains. Leaders who understand this bias can leverage it to motivate their teams by framing goals and objectives in terms of avoiding potential losses rather than focusing solely on potential gains.

Furthermore, behavioral economics emphasizes the power of social norms and context in shaping behavior. Leaders who recognize the influence of social influences can create a positive organizational culture that fosters collaboration, trust, and ethical behavior. By aligning leadership styles with the principles of behavioral economics, leaders can foster a more engaged and motivated workforce, leading to increased productivity and overall organizational success.

In conclusion, behavioral economics offers valuable insights into understanding and improving leadership styles. By acknowledging the biases and cognitive limitations that influence decision-making, leaders can make more informed decisions and create a positive organizational culture. By embracing the principles of behavioral economics, leaders can unleash the power of human behavior and drive success in their organizations.

Team Dynamics and Behavioral Economics

In today's fast-paced and interconnected world, effective teamwork has become essential for organizations to thrive. The ability to work collaboratively and harmoniously with others is crucial for achieving common goals and driving success. However, understanding the dynamics of teams and how human behavior influences their functioning is a complex task. This is where the field of behavioral economics comes into play, providing valuable insights into the intricacies of team dynamics.

Team dynamics refer to the behavioral and psychological processes that occur within a group of individuals working together towards a common objective. These dynamics can significantly impact the team's performance, decision-making, and overall effectiveness. By incorporating principles from behavioral economics, we can gain a deeper understanding of how individual behaviors and biases shape team dynamics.

Behavioral economics focuses on the study of human decision-making and behavior, considering factors such as cognitive biases, social influences, and emotional responses. When applied to team dynamics, behavioral economics helps us comprehend why certain patterns of behavior emerge, how individuals influence each other, and how these dynamics affect the team's outcomes.

One key aspect of team dynamics explored through the lens of behavioral economics is the concept of social norms. People tend to conform to the behaviors and expectations of their peers, often without consciously realizing it. By understanding the power of social norms, team leaders can shape positive behaviors and foster a culture of collaboration and mutual support within their teams.

Another crucial element is the impact of cognitive biases on team decision-making. Behavioral economics has identified numerous biases that can cloud judgment and hinder effective decision-making, such as confirmation bias, anchoring bias, and groupthink. Awareness of these biases can enable teams to mitigate their effects and make more rational and informed choices.

Furthermore, behavioral economics sheds light on the role of incentives in team dynamics. Traditional economic theory assumes that individuals are solely motivated by self-interest. However, behavioral economics recognizes that people are often driven by a mix of intrinsic and extrinsic motivations. By designing incentives that align with the team's objectives and tap into individuals' intrinsic motivations, team leaders can foster higher levels of engagement and productivity.

In conclusion, mastering team dynamics is crucial for success in today's world. By integrating the principles of behavioral economics, we can gain a deeper understanding of the complex interactions that occur within teams. This knowledge allows us to leverage the power of human behavior to create high-performing teams, drive effective decision-making, and enhance organizational outcomes. Whether you are a team leader, a team member, or simply interested in understanding human behavior in group settings, exploring the intersection of team dynamics and behavioral economics is a valuable endeavor.

Harnessing the Power of Diversity in Teams

In today's fast-paced and interconnected world, the ability to effectively manage diverse teams has become an essential skill for successful managers. In this subchapter, we will explore how harnessing the power of diversity in teams can lead to improved performance and innovative solutions.

Diversity in teams extends beyond race, gender, and age. It encompasses a wide range of perspectives, experiences, and backgrounds. Behavioral economics offers valuable insights into how individuals' behaviors and decision-making are influenced by various factors, making it a crucial tool for understanding and leveraging diversity in teams.

One of the key benefits of diversity in teams is the variety of perspectives it brings. When individuals from different backgrounds and with different ways of thinking come together, they bring a wealth of unique insights and ideas. This diversity of perspectives can lead to more creative problem-solving and innovative solutions. By embracing diversity, teams can tap into the collective intelligence and leverage the strengths of each team member.

Moreover, diversity in teams enhances cognitive flexibility. When individuals are exposed to different viewpoints, they are more likely to consider alternative options and think outside the box. This cognitive flexibility enables teams to adapt to changing circumstances and find creative solutions to complex problems. By embracing diversity, managers can foster an environment that encourages open-mindedness and promotes critical thinking.

However, managing diverse teams also comes with its challenges. It requires effective communication, empathy, and a willingness to embrace different viewpoints. Managers need to create an inclusive environment where all team members feel valued and heard. By promoting open dialogue and active listening, managers can harness the power of diversity and create a culture that fosters collaboration and respect.

In conclusion, harnessing the power of diversity in teams is a crucial aspect of mastering management. By leveraging the insights from behavioral economics, managers can understand the impact of diverse perspectives on decision-making and problem-solving. Embracing diversity not only leads to improved team performance but also encourages innovation and creativity. Effective management of diverse teams requires open communication, empathy, and a culture of inclusion. By embracing diversity, managers can unleash the full potential of their teams and achieve extraordinary results.

Chapter 5: Behavioral Economics in Organizational Culture and Change Management

The Role of Culture in Behavioral Economics

Culture plays a significant role in shaping human behavior, and understanding its impact is crucial in the field of behavioral economics. Behavioral economics combines insights from psychology and economics to better understand how people make decisions and behave in various situations. By recognizing the influence of culture, we can gain a deeper understanding of why individuals and groups make certain choices and how culture affects their decision-making processes.

Culture refers to the shared beliefs, values, norms, and practices that characterize a group or society. It shapes our thoughts, emotions, and actions, influencing the way we perceive the world and make choices. Different cultures have their unique ways of interpreting and responding to incentives, which can significantly impact economic decision-making. For instance, some cultures prioritize long-term goals and delayed gratification, while others emphasize immediate rewards and instant gratification.

One key aspect of culture that affects behavioral economics is social norms. These are unwritten rules that govern acceptable behavior within a particular culture or group. Social norms can influence decision-making by shaping our perceptions of what is considered normal or acceptable. For example, in some cultures, saving money is highly valued and seen as a responsible behavior, while in others, spending money lavishly might be the norm.

Cultural differences also influence risk preferences and attitudes towards uncertainty. Some cultures may be more risk-averse, preferring safe and predictable outcomes, while others may be more risk-tolerant and open to uncertainty. These variations in risk preferences can have significant implications for economic decisions such as investment choices or insurance decisions.

Furthermore, culture can impact how individuals respond to incentives and rewards. Different cultures may have varying levels of sensitivity to certain incentives, which can influence their decision-making processes. Understanding these cultural differences can help policymakers and marketers design more effective strategies to influence behavior.

In conclusion, culture plays a crucial role in behavioral economics, shaping our decision-making processes and responses to incentives. Recognizing the influence of culture is essential for understanding human behavior and designing effective interventions. By incorporating cultural factors into the study of behavioral economics, we can gain a more comprehensive understanding of how individuals and groups make choices, and ultimately, unleash the power of human behavior.

Nudging Organizational Culture for Positive Change

In today's fast-paced and competitive business world, organizations are constantly striving to improve their performance and stay ahead of the curve. One powerful tool that can help achieve this is by leveraging the principles of behavioral economics to nudge organizational culture for positive change.

Organizational culture plays a crucial role in shaping employee behavior, decision-making processes, and ultimately, the overall success of a company. By understanding the principles of behavioral economics, organizations can identify the key drivers that influence employee behavior and use this knowledge to create a culture that fosters positive change.

One important aspect of nudging organizational culture is through the use of incentives. Behavioral economics teaches us that people respond to incentives, and organizations can harness this knowledge to encourage desired behaviors. By aligning incentives with the desired cultural values, organizations can motivate employees to adopt behaviors that contribute to a positive and productive workplace.

Another effective way to nudge organizational culture is through the power of social norms. Humans are highly influenced by the behavior of others, and organizations can leverage this inherent tendency to shape cultural norms. By highlighting and celebrating positive behaviors, organizations can create a ripple effect, inspiring others to follow suit and adopt similar behaviors.

Communication also plays a vital role in nudging organizational culture. By effectively communicating the desired cultural values, organizations can help employees understand the importance of these values and how they contribute to the overall success of the company. Clear and consistent communication helps create a shared understanding, fostering a sense of unity and collective responsibility.

Furthermore, leaders play a critical role in shaping organizational culture. By leading by example and embodying the desired cultural values, leaders can inspire and motivate employees to embrace the cultural changes. Leaders can also provide guidance and support to employees as they navigate the transition, ensuring that the desired changes are implemented effectively.

Nudging organizational culture for positive change is not a one-time event but rather an ongoing process. It requires continuous monitoring, feedback, and adaptation to ensure that the desired changes are embedded in the fabric of the organization.

In conclusion, leveraging the principles of behavioral economics can be a powerful tool for organizations looking to nudge their organizational culture for positive change. By aligning incentives, leveraging social norms, improving communication, and empowering leaders, organizations can create a culture that fosters positive behaviors, enhances performance, and ultimately drives success.

Overcoming Resistance to Change through Behavioral Economics

Change is inevitable in life, whether it is in our personal or professional spheres. However, it is also human nature to resist change, often due to fear of the unknown or a desire to maintain the status quo. In the world of management, this resistance can hinder progress and prevent organizations from adapting to new challenges and opportunities. But what if there was a way to understand and address this resistance using the principles of behavioral economics?

In this subchapter, we will explore how behavioral economics can help individuals and organizations overcome resistance to change. Behavioral economics is a field that combines insights from psychology and economics to understand how people make decisions and behave in various contexts. By understanding the underlying biases and heuristics that influence human behavior, we can devise strategies to navigate resistance and facilitate successful change management.

One key concept in behavioral economics is loss aversion, which states that people tend to value avoiding losses more than acquiring equivalent gains. This aversion to loss can create resistance to change, as individuals fear potential negative outcomes. To address this, managers can emphasize the potential benefits of change and highlight the costs of maintaining the status quo. By reframing change as an opportunity for growth and improvement, resistance can be mitigated.

Another principle that can help overcome resistance to change is social proof. People tend to look to others for guidance on how to behave in uncertain situations. By providing social proof of the benefits of change, such as success stories from early adopters or testimonials from respected individuals, managers can influence others to embrace change more readily.

Furthermore, behavioral economics teaches us that people are more motivated by immediate rewards than long-term benefits. By breaking down change into smaller, achievable goals and providing immediate rewards for progress, managers can increase motivation and reduce resistance. This approach taps into our innate desire for instant gratification, making change more appealing and manageable.

In conclusion, behavioral economics provides valuable insights and strategies for overcoming resistance to change. By understanding the biases and heuristics that influence human behavior, managers can effectively navigate resistance and facilitate successful change management. By leveraging concepts such as loss aversion, social proof, and immediate rewards, organizations can overcome resistance, embrace change, and unleash the power of human behavior for growth and success.

Chapter 6: Behavioral Economics in Performance Management and Evaluation

Behavioral Economics and Performance Appraisals

Performance appraisals have long been a staple in the world of management, helping organizations evaluate and reward employee performance. However, traditional approaches to performance appraisals often fall short in capturing the complexities of human behavior and the factors that drive performance. This is where the principles of behavioral economics come into play.

Behavioral economics is a field that combines insights from psychology and economics to understand how people make decisions and behave in various contexts. By incorporating these principles into performance appraisals, organizations can gain a deeper understanding of employee behavior and create more effective evaluation systems.

One key aspect of behavioral economics is the recognition that individuals are not always rational decision-makers. Traditional performance appraisals often assume that employees act purely in their own self-interest, but behavioral economics tells us that human behavior is influenced by a wide range of cognitive biases and social factors. These biases can affect how employees perceive and respond to performance feedback, leading to inaccurate evaluations and missed opportunities for improvement.

By applying the principles of behavioral economics, organizations can design performance appraisal systems that take into account these cognitive biases and social influences. For example, instead of relying solely on numerical ratings or rankings, organizations can incorporate more qualitative feedback that focuses on specific behaviors and outcomes. This approach helps to reduce bias and provides employees with a clearer understanding of their strengths and areas for improvement.

Another important aspect of behavioral economics is the concept of framing. How performance feedback is presented can have a significant impact on how employees perceive and respond to it. By framing feedback in a positive and constructive manner, organizations can motivate employees to strive for improvement and foster a growth mindset. This can lead to increased engagement, productivity, and overall performance.

Furthermore, behavioral economics emphasizes the importance of fairness and equity in performance appraisals. Research has shown that individuals have a strong preference for fairness, and perceptions of fairness can greatly influence employee motivation and satisfaction. By ensuring that performance appraisal processes are transparent, consistent, and free from bias, organizations can promote a sense of fairness and create a positive work environment.

In summary, integrating the principles of behavioral economics into performance appraisals can revolutionize the way organizations evaluate and manage employee performance. By acknowledging the cognitive biases and social influences that shape human behavior, organizations can design more effective appraisal systems that promote fairness, motivation, and continuous improvement. By mastering the principles of behavioral economics, managers and leaders can unleash the power of human behavior and drive organizational success.

Note: This content is written for a general audience interested in the field of behavioral economics, as well as individuals involved in performance appraisal processes within organizations.

Using Behavioral Economics to Improve Performance Feedback

Feedback is a crucial component of personal and professional growth. It helps individuals understand their strengths and weaknesses, identify areas for improvement, and make necessary adjustments to achieve their goals. However, traditional feedback methods often fall short in effectively motivating individuals to enhance their performance. This is where the principles of behavioral economics come into play, offering valuable insights and strategies to optimize the feedback process.

Behavioral economics studies how individuals make decisions and respond to incentives. By understanding the underlying behaviors and biases that influence human decision-making, we can design feedback systems that are more effective in driving positive change. Here are some key principles from behavioral economics that can be applied to improve performance feedback:

1. Framing: The way feedback is presented can greatly impact how it is received and acted upon. By framing feedback in a positive and constructive manner, individuals are more likely to be motivated and receptive to making improvements. Emphasizing progress made and potential growth opportunities can encourage individuals to focus on their strengths and see feedback as a tool for development rather than criticism.

2. Timing: Timely feedback is crucial for individuals to connect their actions with the outcomes they have produced. Behavioral economics suggests that immediate feedback is more effective in influencing behavior change compared to delayed feedback. Providing feedback in

real-time allows individuals to make immediate adjustments and reinforces the connection between their actions and results.

3. Personalization: One size does not fit all when it comes to feedback. Behavioral economics emphasizes the importance of tailoring feedback to individual needs and preferences. By considering individual differences in motivation, learning styles, and cognitive biases, feedback can be customized to maximize its impact and relevance.

4. Incentives and Rewards: Behavioral economics recognizes the power of incentives in shaping behavior. Offering meaningful incentives and rewards can enhance motivation and encourage individuals to strive for higher performance. These can range from monetary bonuses to recognition and praise, aligning with individual preferences and aspirations.

5. Social Norms: Humans are social creatures and are greatly influenced by the behaviors and expectations of those around them. Leveraging social norms in feedback can be a powerful tool to drive performance improvement. By highlighting positive behaviors and achievements of others within a similar context, individuals are more likely to emulate those actions and strive for similar outcomes.

By applying these principles of behavioral economics to performance feedback, organizations and individuals can unlock the full potential of human behavior. By framing feedback positively, delivering it in a timely manner, personalizing it to individual needs, offering incentives and rewards, and leveraging social norms, feedback becomes a powerful tool for growth and development. Mastering the art of performance feedback becomes not just about providing information but about understanding and influencing human behavior.

Designing Effective Performance Incentives

In today's fast-paced and competitive business landscape, organizations are constantly seeking ways to enhance employee performance and drive productivity. One effective tool that has gained significant attention is the use of performance incentives. However, designing effective performance incentives is not an easy task and often requires a deep understanding of human behavior and the principles of behavioral economics.

Behavioral economics combines psychology and economics to understand how individuals make decisions and respond to incentives. By harnessing the power of human behavior, organizations can design performance incentives that truly motivate and engage employees. This subchapter explores the key principles and strategies for designing effective performance incentives, drawing upon the insights from behavioral economics.

One fundamental principle is that incentives should be aligned with individual goals and preferences. People are more likely to be motivated by incentives that are personally meaningful and relevant to their aspirations. By tailoring incentives to individual preferences, organizations can tap into intrinsic motivation and drive higher levels of performance.

Another important principle is that incentives should be tied to measurable and achievable performance metrics. Clear and specific goals enable employees to track their progress and understand how their efforts contribute to the overall success of the organization. Incorporating regular feedback and performance evaluations also enhances the effectiveness of incentives by providing individuals with a sense of accomplishment and recognition.

Additionally, the timing and frequency of incentives play a crucial role in their effectiveness. Behavioral economics suggests that immediate rewards are more impactful than delayed ones. Offering frequent, smaller incentives can create a continuous cycle of motivation and reinforce desired behaviors over time.

Furthermore, the design of incentives should consider the potential for unintended consequences. Behavioral economics highlights the concept of "perverse incentives," where individuals may prioritize short-term gains at the expense of long-term organizational goals. By carefully considering the potential behavioral responses to incentives, organizations can mitigate such risks and ensure that the desired behaviors are encouraged.

In conclusion, designing effective performance incentives requires a deep understanding of human behavior and the principles of behavioral economics. By aligning incentives with individual goals, setting measurable performance metrics, providing timely rewards, and considering potential unintended consequences, organizations can unleash the power of human behavior to drive productivity and enhance employee performance. By mastering the art of designing effective performance incentives, organizations can create a motivated and engaged workforce that propels them towards success in today's competitive business landscape.

Chapter 7: Behavioral Economics in Consumer Behavior and Marketing

Understanding Consumer Decision Making

Consumer decision making lies at the heart of the field of behavioral economics. In this subchapter, we will explore the intricate factors that influence how consumers make decisions and the role that behavioral economics plays in understanding these processes. Whether you are a student, a business professional, or simply someone interested in human behavior, this subchapter will provide valuable insights into the fascinating world of consumer decision making.

Consumer decision making is not a simple linear process. It is influenced by a myriad of factors that can be both conscious and subconscious. Traditional economic theory assumes that individuals make rational decisions based on their preferences and available information. However, behavioral economics challenges this assumption by incorporating psychological and sociological factors into the decision-making process.

One key concept in understanding consumer decision making is the idea of bounded rationality. People have limited cognitive abilities and finite time to make decisions. As a result, they often rely on shortcuts, heuristics, and biases to simplify the decision-making process. These mental shortcuts, while efficient, can sometimes lead to suboptimal decisions.

Furthermore, emotions play a significant role in consumer decision making. Behavioral economics recognizes that individuals are not purely rational beings but are also driven by their emotions, desires, and aspirations. Understanding how emotions shape consumer behavior can help businesses create more effective marketing strategies and products that resonate with their target audience.

Another crucial aspect of consumer decision making is the influence of social and cultural factors. People are influenced by their social networks, peers, and societal norms when making decisions. By understanding these influences, businesses can tailor their marketing efforts to appeal to specific target markets and increase their chances of success.

In this subchapter, we will delve into various theories and models that explain consumer decision making, such as prospect theory, loss aversion, and the theory of planned behavior. We will discuss how these theories can be applied in real-world scenarios and provide practical insights for businesses and marketers.

Understanding consumer decision making is essential for anyone involved in marketing, sales, or product development. By applying the principles of behavioral economics, businesses can gain a deeper understanding of why consumers make certain choices and how to influence those choices effectively.

Whether you are a student looking to expand your knowledge, a business professional seeking new strategies, or simply someone intrigued by human behavior, this subchapter will equip you with valuable insights into the complex world of consumer decision making.

The Influence of Behavioral Economics in Marketing Strategies

In today's fast-paced and competitive business environment, mastering effective marketing strategies is crucial for success. However, traditional marketing techniques often fail to consider the complexities of human behavior and decision-making. This is where the power of behavioral economics comes into play. By understanding how individuals make choices, marketers can unlock the true potential of their campaigns and drive desired consumer behavior.

Behavioral economics is a field that combines insights from psychology and economics to explain why people make certain decisions. It recognizes that humans are not always rational actors, but rather are influenced by a variety of cognitive biases and heuristics. By leveraging these biases, marketers can craft more persuasive messages and design strategies that resonate with consumers on a deeper level.

One key aspect of behavioral economics in marketing is understanding the concept of "nudging." Nudging refers to subtly influencing individuals' decisions without restricting their freedom of choice. By employing nudges, marketers can guide consumers towards certain products or behaviors while still allowing them to feel in control. For example, a supermarket might strategically place healthier snacks at eye level near the checkout counter, making them more likely to be chosen impulsively instead of less healthy alternatives.

Another important principle in behavioral economics is the power of social proof. Humans are highly influenced by the behavior and opinions of others. Marketers can harness this by incorporating social proof elements into their campaigns. Testimonials, user reviews, and endorsements from influencers can all serve as powerful motivators for consumers to choose a particular product or service.

Furthermore, behavioral economics teaches us about the importance of framing and anchoring. The way information is presented can significantly impact decision-making. By framing a product as a limited edition or emphasizing its exclusivity, marketers can create a sense of urgency and desirability. Anchoring, on the other hand, involves presenting a high price or value upfront, which then serves as a reference point for subsequent comparisons. This can make consumers more willing to accept higher prices or perceive greater value.

In conclusion, the influence of behavioral economics in marketing strategies is undeniable. By understanding and leveraging the principles of human behavior, marketers can create more effective campaigns that resonate with consumers and drive desired outcomes. Whether through nudging, social proof, framing, or anchoring, behavioral economics provides valuable insights that can unlock the power of marketing and help businesses thrive in an increasingly competitive marketplace. So, whether you are a seasoned marketer or someone interested in understanding consumer behavior, mastering the principles of behavioral economics is a must.

Nudging Consumers towards Desired Purchases

In today's fast-paced and competitive market, businesses are constantly looking for ways to influence consumer behavior and drive desired purchases. This subchapter explores the fascinating field of behavioral economics and how it can be harnessed to nudge consumers towards making choices that align with their preferences and businesses' objectives.

Behavioral economics combines insights from psychology and economics to understand how people make decisions. It recognizes that consumers are not purely rational actors but are influenced by a range of cognitive biases, emotions, and social factors. By understanding these behavioral patterns, businesses can design strategies and interventions that subtly guide consumers towards desired purchases.

One of the key concepts in behavioral economics is the idea of choice architecture. This refers to how choices are presented and structured, which has a significant impact on decision-making. By strategically designing the environment in which consumers make choices, businesses can nudge them towards certain options. For example, placing popular or higher-margin products at eye level in a store or highlighting limited-time offers can influence consumers to make purchases they might not have considered otherwise.

Another powerful tool in nudging consumers is social proof. People tend to look to others for guidance, especially when faced with uncertainty. By showcasing positive reviews, testimonials, or social media endorsements, businesses can leverage the power of social influence to encourage consumers to make desired purchases. This can be further enhanced by incorporating elements of scarcity, such as limited stock or time-limited offers, to create a sense of urgency and drive purchasing decisions.

However, it is essential to approach nudging ethically and transparently. Consumers should feel empowered and not manipulated by these techniques. Honesty, clarity, and respect for individual autonomy should be at the core of any nudging strategy. Businesses must provide clear information, avoid deceptive tactics, and ensure that consumers are aware of the nudges being used.

In conclusion, behavioral economics offers valuable insights into how businesses can nudge consumers towards desired purchases. By understanding the cognitive biases and behavioral patterns that influence decision-making, businesses can design choice architectures and leverage social proof to guide consumers towards choices that align with their preferences. However, it is crucial to approach nudging ethically and transparently, ensuring that consumers feel empowered and respected throughout the decision-making process.

Chapter 8: Ethical Considerations in Behavioral Economics and Management

Ethical Implications of Nudging in Organizations

In today's world, where organizations are constantly seeking ways to improve productivity and efficiency, the integration of behavioral economics and management has gained significant attention. One powerful tool that has emerged from this collaboration is the concept of nudging – a subtle form of persuasion that aims to influence people's decisions without restricting their freedom of choice. While nudging can be a valuable technique for organizations, it also raises important ethical considerations that must not be ignored.

Nudging operates on the principle that small changes in the way choices are presented can have a significant impact on decision-making. By leveraging insights from behavioral economics, organizations can nudge individuals towards making choices that are in their best interest and align with organizational goals. For example, a company may design its cafeteria layout to encourage healthier eating habits or offer default enrollment in retirement savings plans to promote long-term financial security.

However, the ethical implications of nudging cannot be underestimated. One of the key concerns is the potential for manipulation. Critics argue that nudging can be used to exploit people's biases and vulnerabilities, leading to decisions that may not be in their best interest. It is essential for organizations to ensure that nudges are transparent, respectful of individual autonomy, and do not exploit cognitive biases to manipulate outcomes. Careful consideration must be given to the ethics of the nudges being implemented, ensuring they align with societal norms and values.

Another ethical concern revolves around the potential for unintended consequences. Nudges, even with good intentions, may have unforeseen negative impacts. Organizations must regularly evaluate the outcomes of their nudging strategies to minimize any harm caused and make necessary adjustments. Additionally, individuals should have the ability to opt-out or have alternative choices available, ensuring they are not coerced into decisions that go against their preferences.

To address these ethical concerns, organizations can adopt a set of guiding principles when implementing nudging strategies. These principles may include transparency, choice preservation, informed consent, and continuous evaluation. By adhering to these principles, organizations can ensure that nudging is used responsibly and ethically, benefiting both employees and the organization as a whole.

In conclusion, nudging has emerged as a powerful tool for organizations to influence decision-making and drive positive outcomes. However, its implementation must be accompanied by careful consideration of the ethical implications involved. Organizations must ensure transparency, respect individual autonomy, and regularly evaluate the impact of their nudging strategies. By doing so, they can harness the power of behavioral economics while upholding ethical standards, contributing to a more responsible and effective approach to management.

Ensuring Fairness and Transparency in Behavioral Economics Strategies

In the realm of behavioral economics, it is essential to prioritize fairness and transparency in the strategies employed. The study of human behavior is a powerful tool that can shape decision-making processes and influence outcomes. However, without a commitment to fairness and transparency, these strategies can inadvertently lead to biased or manipulative practices.

Fairness is a fundamental aspect of any behavioral economics strategy. It involves treating individuals equitably and avoiding any form of discrimination or bias. Whether it is in designing experiments or implementing interventions, fairness should be at the forefront of decision-making. By ensuring fairness, behavioral economists can create an environment that promotes trust, credibility, and cooperation among individuals.

Transparency is equally crucial in behavioral economics strategies. It involves disclosing information openly and honestly, allowing individuals to make informed decisions. Transparency ensures that individuals understand the underlying principles and motivations behind the strategies employed. By being transparent, behavioral economists can build credibility and foster a sense of accountability.

To ensure fairness and transparency in behavioral economics strategies, several guidelines can be followed. First and foremost, it is crucial to establish clear objectives and communicate them to all stakeholders involved. By outlining the purpose and expected outcomes, individuals can understand the intentions behind the strategies employed.

Additionally, behavioral economists should strive to include diverse perspectives and ensure representation from various demographic groups. This inclusivity helps to minimize biases and ensures that strategies are designed to benefit a wide range of individuals rather than a select few.

Furthermore, conducting thorough and unbiased research is essential. Rigorous experimentation and data analysis are paramount to ensure that the strategies employed are based on sound evidence rather than assumptions or personal biases. By adhering to scientific principles, behavioral economists can enhance the credibility and reliability of their strategies.

Lastly, regular evaluation and feedback are crucial to ensure ongoing fairness and transparency. By soliciting feedback from individuals affected by the strategies, behavioral economists can make necessary adjustments and address any concerns that arise. This iterative process helps to refine strategies and ensure that they continue to meet the needs and expectations of the target audience.

In conclusion, fairness and transparency are vital components of behavioral economics strategies. By prioritizing these principles, behavioral economists can create interventions that promote trust, credibility, and cooperation among individuals. By establishing clear objectives, including diverse perspectives, conducting unbiased research, and seeking regular feedback, fairness and transparency can be ensured in the field of behavioral economics.

Balancing Ethical Concerns with Organizational Objectives

In the dynamic world of business, organizations face a multitude of challenges when it comes to achieving their objectives while maintaining ethical standards. This subchapter aims to explore the concept of balancing ethical concerns with organizational objectives through the lens of behavioral economics.

Behavioral economics, a field that combines insights from psychology and economics, provides a unique perspective on understanding human behavior in the context of decision-making. By analyzing the cognitive biases and heuristics that influence individuals' choices, behavioral economics sheds light on how organizations can navigate the ethical landscape effectively.

Ethical concerns arise when organizations encounter dilemmas that test the moral fabric of their decision-making processes. Often, organizations may face the temptation to prioritize profit maximization at the expense of ethical considerations. However, this shortsighted approach can lead to severe consequences, including damage to reputation, legal issues, and loss of public trust.

To strike a balance between ethical concerns and organizational objectives, it is crucial for organizations to adopt a behavioral economics mindset. This entails understanding the psychological factors that influence decision-making within the organization and designing systems that promote ethical behavior.

One key aspect of this approach is the acknowledgment of cognitive biases that can lead individuals astray from ethical choices. By identifying and addressing these biases, organizations can create an environment that encourages ethical decision-making. For instance, implementing ethical guidelines, providing training on ethical behavior, and fostering an open culture that encourages employees to voice concerns can help mitigate biases and promote ethical conduct.

Moreover, organizations can leverage behavioral economics principles to align individual and organizational goals. Incentive structures, for instance, can be designed to reward ethical behavior and discourage unethical practices. By integrating ethical considerations into performance evaluations and compensation systems, organizations can create a strong link between ethical conduct and individual success.

To ensure the longevity and sustainability of their organizations, leaders must recognize that ethical concerns are not obstacles to success but rather essential components of it. By embracing the insights of behavioral economics and incorporating ethical considerations into their decision-making processes, organizations can create a win-win situation, where ethical behavior and organizational objectives go hand in hand.

In conclusion, the balancing act between ethical concerns and organizational objectives is a critical challenge faced by every organization. By adopting a behavioral economics approach, organizations can navigate this delicate terrain more effectively. This subchapter has explored the importance of understanding cognitive biases, designing systems that promote ethical behavior, and aligning individual and organizational goals. By doing so, organizations can unleash the power of human behavior, ensuring long-term success while upholding ethical principles.

Chapter 9: Implementing Behavioral Economics in Organizational Practices

Building a Behavioral Economics Framework in Organizations

In today's fast-paced and competitive business landscape, organizations are increasingly recognizing the importance of understanding human behavior to drive success. Behavioral economics, a field that combines psychology and economics, provides valuable insights into how individuals make decisions and can be a powerful tool for organizations to optimize their operations.

This subchapter aims to guide organizations in building a behavioral economics framework, allowing them to harness the power of human behavior to achieve their goals. Whether you are a business owner, manager, or employee, understanding the principles of behavioral economics can benefit you and your organization.

The first step in building a behavioral economics framework is to gain a deep understanding of the underlying principles. This includes understanding concepts such as cognitive biases, heuristics, and prospect theory. By recognizing how these principles affect decision-making processes, organizations can design strategies that align with human behavior and drive desired outcomes.

Next, organizations should gather data to identify patterns and trends in human behavior within their specific context. This can be done through surveys, experiments, or analysis of existing data. By collecting and analyzing this information, organizations can gain valuable insights into the factors that influence behavior within their organization and industry.

Once the data is collected, organizations can begin implementing interventions based on behavioral economics principles. These interventions can be as simple as changing the way information is presented or as complex as restructuring incentive systems. By aligning these interventions with the identified patterns and trends, organizations can nudge individuals towards desired behaviors and outcomes.

It is important to note that building a behavioral economics framework is an ongoing process. Organizations should continuously monitor and evaluate the effectiveness of their interventions and make adjustments as needed. This iterative approach allows organizations to learn from their experiences and refine their strategies over time.

Ultimately, building a behavioral economics framework in organizations can lead to improved decision-making, increased employee engagement, and greater customer satisfaction. By understanding and leveraging human behavior, organizations can unlock the power of behavioral economics and gain a competitive advantage in today's dynamic business environment.

In conclusion, this subchapter on building a behavioral economics framework provides a comprehensive guide for organizations to leverage the principles of human behavior to drive success. Whether you are a business owner, manager, or employee, understanding and applying the principles of behavioral economics can lead to improved outcomes and enhanced organizational performance. By continuously learning, adapting, and refining strategies based on human behavior, organizations can thrive in today's complex and ever-changing business landscape.

Strategies for Integrating Behavioral Economics into Management Processes

In today's rapidly evolving business landscape, understanding human behavior has become crucial for effective management. Behavioral economics, a field that combines psychology and economics, provides valuable insights into the decision-making processes of individuals and groups. By incorporating behavioral economics into management processes, organizations can unlock the power of human behavior to drive success and achieve their goals. This subchapter explores strategies for integrating behavioral economics into management processes, enabling managers from all industries and backgrounds to harness the potential of this field.

One strategy is to use behavioral insights to design effective incentive systems. Traditional incentive systems often rely solely on financial rewards, assuming that individuals are solely motivated by monetary gains. However, behavioral economics suggests that other factors, such as social recognition and intrinsic motivation, significantly influence behavior. By understanding these additional motivators, managers can design more tailored and effective incentive systems that resonate with their employees, resulting in increased productivity and satisfaction.

Another strategy involves applying behavioral economic principles to decision-making processes. Traditional decision-making models assume rationality, yet human behavior is rarely purely rational. By incorporating insights from behavioral economics, managers can account for cognitive biases and heuristics that can impact decision-making. For example, understanding the concept of "loss aversion" can help managers frame decisions in a way that minimizes perceived losses, increasing buy-in and acceptance from employees.

Furthermore, integrating behavioral economics into management processes can help promote ethical behavior within organizations. By understanding the psychological factors that drive unethical behavior, managers can create environments that discourage such conduct. Strategies such as promoting a strong ethical culture, providing clear guidelines, and implementing transparency measures can help align employee behavior with ethical standards.

Additionally, managers can leverage behavioral economics to enhance customer engagement and satisfaction. By understanding consumer behavior and decision-making processes, organizations can design products, services, and marketing campaigns that better resonate with their target audience. This approach can lead to increased customer loyalty, higher sales, and improved brand reputation.

In conclusion, integrating behavioral economics into management processes offers numerous benefits across various industries and niches. By applying the insights from this field, managers can design more effective incentive systems, make better decisions, promote ethical behavior, and enhance customer engagement. As organizations strive to unlock the power of human behavior, mastering management with behavioral economics becomes imperative for success in the modern business world.

Overcoming Challenges in Implementing Behavioral Economics

Behavioral economics is a fascinating field that combines insights from psychology and economics to understand and influence human behavior. It has gained significant attention in recent years, as organizations and policymakers recognize its potential to improve decision-making processes and outcomes. However, like any new approach, implementing behavioral economics can come with its fair share of challenges. In this subchapter, we will explore some of these challenges and offer strategies to overcome them.

One of the primary challenges in implementing behavioral economics is overcoming resistance to change. Traditional economic theories have long dominated decision-making processes, and introducing a new approach can be met with skepticism and resistance. To overcome this challenge, it is important to communicate the benefits of behavioral economics effectively. Highlight how it can enhance decision-making, improve outcomes, and create a more comprehensive understanding of human behavior.

Another challenge is the complexity of human behavior itself. While traditional economic theories often assume rationality, behavioral economics recognizes that humans are not always rational decision-makers. Understanding the nuances of human behavior requires a multidisciplinary approach, incorporating insights from psychology, sociology, and neuroscience. Overcoming this challenge involves building a strong foundation of knowledge in these areas and continually updating and expanding your understanding.

A key challenge in implementing behavioral economics is the availability of data. Behavioral economics relies heavily on data to identify patterns and make informed decisions. However, collecting accurate and relevant data can be a significant hurdle. To overcome this challenge, it is important to invest in data collection methods and technologies that capture behavioral insights effectively. This may involve leveraging new technologies such as machine learning and artificial intelligence to collect and analyze large datasets.

Lastly, implementing behavioral economics requires a shift in mindset and culture. It is not enough to simply adopt new techniques and frameworks; organizations must foster a culture that values and embraces behavioral economics principles. This involves training employees, creating incentives that align with behavioral economics principles, and empowering individuals to make decisions based on behavioral insights.

In conclusion, while implementing behavioral economics can be challenging, the benefits are well worth the effort. By overcoming resistance to change, understanding the complexities of human behavior, investing in data collection methods, and fostering a culture that embraces behavioral economics, organizations can unleash the power of human behavior and improve decision-making processes and outcomes. It is an exciting journey that requires continuous learning and adaptation, but the rewards are immense. So, let us embrace the challenges and embark on this transformative journey towards mastering management with behavioral economics.

Chapter 10: The Future of Behavioral Economics in Organizational Behavior and Management

Advancements in Behavioral Economics Research

Behavioral economics is a fascinating field that combines traditional economic theories with insights from psychology and other social sciences to understand and predict human behavior in the realm of decision-making. Over the years, significant advancements have been made in this field, leading to a deeper understanding of why people make the choices they do and how their behavior can be influenced.

One of the most important advancements in behavioral economics research is the recognition that humans are not always rational decision-makers. Traditional economic theory assumes that individuals always act in their own self-interest and make decisions based on full and complete information. However, research in behavioral economics has shown that people often deviate from this rational model due to cognitive biases and heuristics.

Cognitive biases refer to systematic errors in thinking that can lead to irrational decision-making. For example, the availability bias occurs when people rely on immediate examples or vivid information to make judgments, disregarding statistical data. Another important cognitive bias is the framing effect, which demonstrates that people's decisions can be influenced by how information is presented to them.

Heuristics, on the other hand, are mental shortcuts or rules of thumb that individuals use to simplify decision-making. These shortcuts can be helpful in certain situations, but they can also lead to biases and errors. For instance, the anchoring bias occurs when people rely heavily on the first piece of information they receive when making a decision, even if it is irrelevant or arbitrary.

Advancements in behavioral economics research have also shed light on the role of emotions in decision-making. Traditional economic theory assumes that individuals are purely rational, but research has shown that emotions play a significant role in shaping our choices. For example, studies have demonstrated that individuals are more likely to take risks when they are in a positive emotional state, leading to potentially irrational decisions.

Furthermore, advancements in technology and data analysis have allowed researchers to conduct large-scale experiments and gather real-time data on human behavior. This has enabled a more comprehensive understanding of decision-making in various contexts, ranging from financial markets to health-related choices.

In conclusion, the field of behavioral economics has made significant advancements in understanding human decision-making. By recognizing the limitations of traditional economic theory and incorporating insights from psychology, cognitive science, and other disciplines, researchers have uncovered the complex nature of human behavior. This knowledge has practical implications for a wide range of fields, including marketing, public policy, and organizational management. As our understanding of behavioral economics continues to evolve, it holds the potential to revolutionize how we approach and influence human behavior in various settings.

Potential Applications and Innovations

Behavioral economics has revolutionized the way we understand human behavior and decision-making. By integrating insights from psychology and economics, this field has provided valuable tools for understanding and predicting human behavior in a wide range of contexts. In this subchapter, we will explore the potential applications and innovations of behavioral economics and how they can be harnessed to unleash the power of human behavior.

One of the key areas where behavioral economics has found application is in the field of marketing and advertising. By understanding the cognitive biases and heuristics that influence consumer decision-making, marketers can design more effective strategies to influence consumer behavior. For example, the use of social proof and scarcity can create a sense of urgency and increase the likelihood of purchase. Furthermore, the concept of framing can be used to present information in a way that influences consumer choices.

In the realm of public policy, behavioral economics has the potential to tackle some of the most pressing social issues. By understanding the factors that drive human behavior, policymakers can design interventions that nudge people towards making better choices. For instance, behavioral interventions have been successfully used to promote healthy behaviors such as exercise and healthy eating. By leveraging insights from behavioral economics, policymakers can create environments that make it easier for individuals to make optimal choices.

Another exciting application of behavioral economics is in the field of finance. Traditional economic models assume that individuals always make rational decisions, but behavioral economics recognizes that humans are prone to biases and irrational behavior. By taking these factors into account, financial institutions can develop better investment strategies and improve risk management. Moreover, behavioral economics can help individuals make better financial decisions by providing insights into saving, investing, and retirement planning.

Innovation is also a key aspect of behavioral economics. Researchers are constantly discovering new biases and heuristics that influence human behavior. By understanding these cognitive processes, businesses can develop innovative solutions to address consumer needs and preferences. For example, companies can design user-friendly apps that align with individuals' cognitive biases, making it easier for them to achieve their goals.

In conclusion, behavioral economics has immense potential in various domains. Its applications range from marketing and public policy to finance and innovation. By harnessing the power of human behavior, we can create more effective strategies, design better policies, and make smarter financial decisions. Behavioral economics truly has the potential to unlock the hidden forces that shape our behavior and pave the way for a more prosperous and sustainable future for everyone.

Embracing Behavioral Economics for Sustainable Organizational Success

In today's competitive business landscape, organizations are constantly seeking ways to gain a competitive edge and achieve sustainable success. One powerful tool that has emerged in recent years is behavioral economics. This field combines psychology and economics to understand how individuals make decisions and how these decisions impact their behavior.

For everyone, from business leaders to individual contributors, understanding and applying the principles of behavioral economics can lead to improved decision-making, increased productivity, and ultimately, sustainable organizational success.

At its core, behavioral economics challenges the traditional assumptions of rational decision-making. It acknowledges that humans are not always rational actors but are instead influenced by a variety of biases, heuristics, and social factors. By embracing these insights, organizations can design more effective policies, processes, and strategies that align with human behavior.

One key aspect of behavioral economics is the concept of nudges. Nudges are subtle changes in the environment that can influence individuals' behavior without restricting their freedom of choice. For example, placing healthy snacks at eye level in the office cafeteria can nudge employees towards making healthier food choices. By understanding how to design effective nudges, organizations can promote positive behaviors and drive sustainable change.

Another important principle of behavioral economics is the power of social norms. Humans are highly influenced by what others are doing, and by leveraging this knowledge, organizations can shape desired behaviors. For instance, publicizing the energy-saving habits of employees can encourage others to follow suit, leading to a more sustainable workplace.

Furthermore, behavioral economics emphasizes the importance of framing and context in decision-making. By presenting information in a certain way, organizations can influence how individuals perceive and interpret it. For example, highlighting the potential losses instead of gains can motivate employees to take action and avoid potential risks.

To truly harness the power of behavioral economics, organizations must adopt a data-driven approach. By collecting and analyzing data on individual behavior and decision-making patterns, organizations can identify trends, understand what motivates their employees, and tailor interventions accordingly. This evidence-based approach empowers organizations to make informed decisions and design effective strategies for sustainable success.

In conclusion, embracing behavioral economics is crucial for organizations aiming for sustainable success. By understanding human behavior and applying the principles of behavioral economics, organizations can design policies, processes, and strategies that align with how individuals actually make decisions. Nudges, social norms, framing, and data-driven insights all play a significant role in driving sustainable change. By embracing behavioral economics, organizations can unleash the power of human behavior and achieve long-term success in today's complex business landscape.

Conclusion: Unleashing the Power of Human Behavior through Behavioral Economics in Management and Organizational Behavior

In this book, "Mastering Management with Behavioral Economics: Unleashing the Power of Human Behavior," we have explored the fascinating world of behavioral economics and its applications in management and organizational behavior. Throughout this journey, we have discovered how understanding and leveraging human behavior can lead to improved decision-making, increased productivity, and enhanced overall performance.

Behavioral economics provides a fresh lens through which we can view the complexities of human behavior in the workplace. By integrating insights from psychology, sociology, and economics, this field allows us to understand why people make certain choices and how their behavior can be influenced. It challenges traditional economic assumptions that humans are always rational and self-interested actors, instead recognizing the importance of cognitive biases, social norms, and emotions in decision-making processes.

In the realm of management, behavioral economics offers valuable tools for effectively leading and motivating employees. By recognizing that individuals are not always driven solely by financial incentives, managers can design more effective reward systems that align with employees' psychological needs. Furthermore, understanding the role of social norms and peer influence can help create a positive work culture that fosters cooperation and collaboration.

Organizational behavior is another area where behavioral economics can revolutionize our understanding. By acknowledging the bounded rationality of individuals, organizations can design decision-making processes that account for cognitive limitations and biases. This can lead to better strategic planning, risk management, and innovation within the organization. Additionally, behavioral economics sheds light on the influence of emotions and ethical considerations on employee behavior, allowing organizations to create environments that promote well-being and ethical conduct.

For everyone interested in behavioral economics, this book has aimed to provide an accessible introduction to the field and its applications in management and organizational behavior. By incorporating the principles and insights from behavioral economics into our daily practices, we can unlock the true potential of human behavior and drive positive change within ourselves, our teams, and our organizations.

Remember, the power of behavioral economics lies not just in understanding human behavior but also in leveraging that knowledge to create more effective management strategies, foster better organizational behavior, and ultimately achieve greater success. By embracing the principles of behavioral economics, we can unleash the power of human behavior and create thriving workplaces where individuals and organizations can thrive together.

Printed in the USA
CPSIA information can be obtained
at www.ICGtesting.com
LVHW011340220624
783639LV00011B/541

9 798869 045546